PowerKids Readers:
Nature Books™

Fruits

Jacqueline Dwyer

The Rosen Publishing Group's
PowerKids Press™
New York

Published in 2001 by The Rosen Publishing Group, Inc.
29 East 21st Street, New York, NY 10010

First Edition

Book Design: Michael de Guzman
Layout: Felicity Erwin and Nicholas Sciacca

Photo Credits: pp. 1, 7, 9, 15 © UNIPHOTO Picture Agency; pp. 5, 11, 13, 21 © SuperStock; p. 17 © F.P.G./Dennie Cody; p. 19 © UNIPHOTO Picture Agency/Frank Siteman; p. 22 (field, tree) © SuperStock.

Dwyer, Jackie, 1970–
    Fruits / by Jacqueline Dwyer.
        p. cm.— (PowerKids readers nature books)
    Summary: Examines different fruits and how they are grown, picked, and packaged.
    ISBN 0-8239-5678-4 (lib. bdg. : alk. paper)
    1. Fruit—Juvenile literature. [1. Fruit. 2. Fruit culture.] I. Title.

SB357.2 .D88 2000
634—dc21   99-049795

Manufactured in the United States of America

Contents

Fruits are many different shapes, sizes, and colors. Fruit is the juicy part of a plant that we eat.

All seeds need water and sunlight to grow. Most fruit starts out as seeds. The seeds grow into new fruit plants.

7

Pears are fruit that grow on trees.

9

Blackberries are fruit that grow on bushes.

Strawberries are fruit that grow in a field.

Oranges are citrus fruit. Citrus fruits are also called sunshine fruits. Citrus fruits grow where it is warm and sunny.

Tractors are used to pick fruit. Grapes are picked by a tractor that shakes the grapevine. The grapes fall into the big tractor.

Apples are packed in boxes. The boxes of apples are loaded onto a truck. The truck takes the apples to the store.

19

Watermelon is a fruit.
Fruit is good for you. Fruit
tastes great, too. It's a
good idea to eat fruit
every day.

21

Words to Know

FIELD

PLANT

SEEDS

TRACTOR

TREE

Here are more books to read about fruits:
The First Book of Fruits
By Barbara L. Beck
Franklin Watts, Inc.

Hooray for Orchards!
By Bobbie Kalman
Crabtree Publishing Company

To learn more about fruits, check out this Web site:
http://www.dole.com/

Index

Word Count: 149

Note to Librarians, Teachers, and Parents

PowerKids Readers (Nature Books) are specially designed to help emergent and beginning readers build their skills in reading for information. Simple vocabulary and concepts are paired with photographs of real kids in real-life situations or stunning, detailed images from the natural world around them. Readers will respond to written language by linking meaning with their own everyday experiences and observations. Sentences are short and simple, employing a basic vocabulary of sight words, as well as new words that describe objects or processes that take place in the natural world. Large type, clean design, and photographs corresponding directly to the text all help children to decipher meaning. Features such as a contents page, picture glossary, and index help children get the most out of PowerKids Readers. They also introduce children to the basic elements of a book, which they will encounter in their future reading experiences. Lists of related books and Web sites encourage kids to explore other sources and to continue the process of learning.